AFTER THE EQUINOX
COSTAS NISIOTIS

For Colette Payerne
(1954-2008)
and our sons, Nikolas and Theophile

Shoestring Press

Printed by imprintdigital
Upton Pyne, Exeter
www.imprintdigital.net

Typeset by narrator
www.narrator.me.uk
enquiries@narrator.me.uk

Published by Shoestring Press
19 Devonshire Avenue, Beeston, Nottingham, NG9 1BS
(0115) 925 1827
www.shoestringpress.co.uk

First published 2011
© Copyright: Costas Nisiotis
The moral right of the author has been asserted.
ISBN 978 1 907356 41 4

IN PRAISE OF A CITY

London forged me.
It taught me queuing, commuting and socializing
at launderettes.
It taught me Arabic greetings and lunchtime concerts.
It taught me lawns and lanes at weekends and a neat
network of streets that always led home.
It taught me parenthood and nursery rhymes
and things too dear and too trivial to list.
It taught me PET scans and palliative care units.
It taught me loss.

I REMEMBER

We held the hands of our children
as though the beatings of our hearts
depended on that clasp.
We held fast to the infinite security
those small hands gave.
We never told them.
Never said how much they strengthened us
how much they fed in us the need of love
how much we needed that need.

THEN

I was always on the move like a wandering Jew
seeking affordable lodgings.
All I owned fitted in a suitcase.
Rented rooms with a view of backyards and railway lines
slept on mattresses sullied with intimacy
read behind curtains that were columns of dust.
Yet those student years were full of sun
full of tomorrow.

BLOOMSBURY 2008

"Jesus loves you"
said the stranger with a smile
as he rushed past my grief
in Bloomsbury.
I was bereft. I had no time to thank
your blonde apostle, Lord.
Please thank him.

DREAD

"There's nothing we can do for you."

The dread of abandon raises a wall between you
and the light.
It immures you alive.
Those you love cry at the wall.
You feel sorry for them
If sorry can fathom the *Sorrow*
if Sorrow can sound the Despair.
You want life, blue skies and elderberry blossoms.
But the wall hides all
the sky, the blossoms and the prayers.

EVENING RAIN

Our children will lull us to sleep one day
and the dogs that grew old with us
will lick our fingers.
The days will be short
the rain will tap on our walls
and we shall hear it loud on the window panes.
The trees will shine black in their loneliness
but we, no, we will not be alone:
Tucked under the blanket, with a hot cup of tea
on the bedside table and their hands
on our forehead
we will swallow their fantastic tales and dream
of gardens with round ponds and nonchalant
swans.
And sleep will slowly descend upon us
and our dog will surrender first
and the light will become dim
and the rain will cease
and our children cover us
tenderly, fatherly, with a farewell.

CREDO

To my sons

I believe in two gods who never divide me.
I have broken the tablets and the Ten Commandments
and in my boundless conceit stood as my own prophet.
I know these gods well
I see them eye to eye, speak to them loudly
but without irreverence
and in my silence I feel their judgment
a light lucid rain.
Jeremiah would have been a sheep
and Job a very happy shepherd
had they believed in my two gods
who suffered and still forgive.

FORGIVENESS

Forgiveness springs
from soft coral sprouts
and fills the sea of rage
with columns of light.

PASCAL

I had the privilege to be born twice.
On June 19, 1623 in Clermont Ferrand
and on November 23, 1654 in Neuilly
Monday between ten and midnight.
Theorems distracted me and I kept forgetting
my feet that froze, the gut that burnt.
Yet, that November night a Spirit lifted my body
over illness and the world.
"God of Abraham, God of Isaac, God of Jacob,
not of the philosophers and sages."
For two full hours I throbbed in the flame
that illuminated the night of my soul.
"Certitude, certitude. Emotion. Joy. Peace."
My hand trembled as I wrote.
My eyes, weary from treatises, welled with tears.
"Joy, joy, joy. Tears of joy."
The scale of numbers had taken me away.
"I avoided Him, I denied Him, I crucified Him."
I wept profusely. I swore "never to leave Him."
The words my heart wrote that night are my talisman
God of my salvation, God of Pascal!

Phrases in quotes from the note that was found in Pascal's gown.

PLAIN GRAMMAR

There are no rules of syntax
in the grammar of loss.
Just a few cruel tenses
and a desolate verb
in first person declensions.

NOISELESS WORK

Sorrow exerts a taciturn dominion.
It builds itself within.
Nothing visible, nothing audible.
The cocoon grows despite itself
the sacred worm weaves its thread
in the void.
Thus the thread.
Thus the veil.
Thus the indestructible silk.

DESCARTES

I, René Descartes, defined space.
My axes pierce the universe.
Even the most insignificant point
gives a triple account.
Even the most infinitesimal shift
is registered by my coordinates.
Outside it's dark.
Under the candelabra Christina gave me
glow the rule and the compass.
I feel my soul heavy.
Meditation saddens me.
I long for the flat, the plane
and the square
that keeps me prisoner in its grid.

IMPROMPTU

The poem you jotted down in the café
and rewrote on the Tube
will outlive you even if your soul
fails heaven's entry requirements.
Ink and paper know no metaphysics.
Nor does the coffee you sipped
while writing these lines
or the smiling Ukrainian waitress
or the linden tree.
They are all very much of this world
yet they give you eternal moments.

A TOKEN OF GRATITUDE FOR

all things small
the chemistry that put together
22 Park Place East
my mother and father
the promise of two sons
the lavender in the flowerbeds
in Luxembourg
the dawns that will come.

CORE VALUE

It is not metaphor
that makes the poem
nor metre
nor even meaning
but your primitive heart.

MERCENARY

Carpe diem!
Not the common calendar diem
you tear off the wall
nor the red anniversary diem
you habitually forget
but the golden opportunity diem
when despair cries for help
misery for shelter
and famine for a few crumbs.
Go on! Seize that diem!
Build your Rome in a day!

THE DEPARTURE

My father died on a wintry Sunday afternoon.
Moments before, his hair became black and curly
his eyes bright green. On his left wrist appeared
the watch with the gold bracelet.
He glanced at it and sprang out of bed.
A white shirt hung by the bedside.
He tucked it into black trousers.
"Not the black suit again?" I protested.
"That's the suit I got married in.
The room smells like a clinic. Open the windows
wide. Give the wheelchair to an Old People's Home."
"Are you sad you're leaving?" I asked him.
"The Equator divides my world into two equal parts:
the joy of seeing your mother and the sorrow
of leaving you. I'm about to cross it."
I knelt and hugged him. Then my father left.

AFTER THE EQUINOX

I am looking for an endless road
lined with linden trees
with pavements I can walk unhampered
by regrets for the people I have hurt
a road I can tread without thought
a road I know does not exist
a road that incessantly leads me on.

WHEN THE LIGHTS GO OUT

When the lights go out
and all of us are plunged into darkness
perhaps then we may call to mind
what we have forgotten:
how to listen carefully
how to tread cautiously
asking for pardon
with every step we take
how to see with eyes wide open.

SIMON OF CYRENE

I took pride in my strength
felt my shoulders could lift cedars.
Mother and need made me sturdy
or a certain fate.
I grew up amid god-fearing folk and learnt fear.
I was tall and had to duck among the crowd
that day
but the Roman grabbed me
and ordered me to carry the cross.

Now I have something to remember
when all strength fails me
something that will weigh on my back
until I close my eyes
something I owe to you, Centurion.

TO ALL POETS

Take your best poem
seal it in a bottle
throw it in the sea.
Trust the vastness.

RECYCLING

Words our tongue has corroded
are not left to die in dignity
on some remote skeleton coast.
Instead, they are electroplated
and electrified into sleek slogans
just below the brand
just above the health warning.

THE SIGN

In golden gothic characters
under the clock in Ghent's railway station:
Fugit irreparabile Tempus.
The maxim seared itself in my mind.
How did the clock know about our visit?
The surgery all hope clung to?
The invader had nothing to fear.
"My name is legion for we are many."

The surgery erased hope.
Fugit irreparabile Tempus.
The legion loots and plunders.
Now that I write, at three in the morning,
the plundering goes on unabated.

And the boys?
The joys you will not see?
Mercy!
"There is no mercy. My name is legion."

On the station clock
the hour hand follows the minute hand
without the least remorse.

UNWRITTEN

However many poems you write
one will always remain unwritten.
It is the poem that writhes inside you
the poem your shadows whisper
the poem you cannot escape from.

THE BETRAYED

With the noose round my neck
I set off for the olive grove.
I wanted to choose the tree *myself*
not the God who cursed me with silver.
Why did it fall to me?
Why not Matthew the tax collector?
Why not Thomas the doubter?
Why not Peter who renounced Him
three times?
I was the lamb of Jesus. Now I walk
to my death knowing there is no resurrection.
Men will forever condemn me
yet I believed in Him without a shadow
of a doubt.

THE FAILURE OF ALCHEMY

He worked to transmute tones
of grief into a few lines.
He gave himself to the cause.

Grief resisted him.
He persisted.

The grief was intrasmutable.

YOUR POETRY

From the cracks of an agony
you thought hermetic
springs a poetry that speaks to you
that only for you has meaning.
It wants to save you from disintegration
it aspires to nothing else.

OLD HOUSES

To Alex Martin

The walls of old houses are thick.
Stones stacked one above the other
held in place by their own weight
timbers wedged horizontally and vertically
to hold the windows and let in light
and the night.
The floors groan under footfalls,
through gaps between shrunken floorboards
coins of forgotten currencies slip into the safe hollows
of the house.
Ah, if only you had been able to hide your florins!
Where did you put them?
You ransack pockets, drawers, cupboards,
the rooms upstairs. Nowhere.
You knew you wouldn't find them. You wanted to be sure.
You live so much in memory you are puzzled
by each gleam that catches your eye.
No. Your florins have been spent well.
The gardens of old houses soonest run to weeds.
Cats stretch out in their grass and bees gather
the harvest of their wild flowers.

LOVE

Why do I want to write about my loved ones
who are no longer here?
They wouldn't want it.
They wanted to give and they gave
and forgot what they gave.
They never took nor claimed anything.
They were gifts themselves.

PARTICLE PHYSICS

The Poet is anti-matter
in the stream of the accelerator.
He collides with matter
and produces light.